Simple
Steps

Also by Bill Hybels

Becoming a Contagious Christian
(with Mark Mittelberg and Lee Strobel)

Courageous Leadership

Descending into Greatness (with Rob Wilkins)

Fit to Be Tied (with Lynne Hybels)

Holy Discontent

Honest to God?

Rediscovering Church (with Lynne Hybels)

The Volunteer Revolution

The New Community Series
(with Kevin and Sherry Harney)

Colossians
James
1 Peter
Philippians
Romans
The Sermon on the Mount 1
The Sermon on the Mount 2

The InterActions Small Group Series
(with Kevin and Sherry Harney)

Authenticity
Character
Commitment
Community
Essential Christianity
Fruit of the Spirit
Getting a Grip
Jesus
Lessons on Love
Living in God's Power

Love in Action
Marriage
Meeting God
New Identity
Parenting
Prayer
Reaching Out
The Real Deal
Significance
Transformation

BILL HYBELS

Simple Steps

POINTING PEOPLE TO FAITH

ZONDERVAN.com/
AUTHORTRACKER
follow your favorite authors

Simple Steps
Copyright © 2006, 2007 by Bill Hybels

Requests for information should be addressed to:

Zondervan, *Grand Rapids, Michigan 49530*

ISBN-13: 978-0-310-61034-3
ISBN-10: 0-310-61034-6

All Scripture quotations, unless otherwise indicated, are taken from the *Holy Bible: Today's New International Version*®. TNIV®. Copyright © 2001, 2004 by International Bible Society. Used by permission of Zondervan. All rights reserved.

For Scripture quotations from *The Message*: Copyright © by Eugene H. Peterson 1993, 1994, 1995, 1996, 2000, 2001, 2002. Used by permission of NavPress Publishing Group.

The website addresses recommended throughout this book are offered as a resource to you. These websites are not intended in any way to be or imply an endorsement on the part of Zondervan, nor do we vouch for their content for the life of this book.

Interior design by Beth Shagene

Printed in the United States of America

07 08 09 10 11 12 13 • 15 14 13 12 11 10 9 8 7 6 5 4 3 2 1

Contents

CHAPTER 1

The Ultimate Walk Across a Room

Ten thousand steps.

Roughly, that's the distance you travel sunrise to sunset, each and every day of your life. It adds up to about 115,000 miles in a lifetime — or more than four times around this big blue planet of ours.*

With that said, just one question: Are you using your steps wisely?

Assume the average distance across most rooms is twenty feet — about ten steps. The question I hope to answer is this: What if ten steps — just one one-thousandth of your daily average — could actually impact eternity?

If so, it might well change the way you walk.

The concept surfaced many months ago after I attended a lunch in a southern state. Hundreds of us representing a variety of ethnicities gathered in a hotel ballroom, and I sensed I was in for an interesting experience. As the rest of my table convened, I would discover that our diversity went beyond race to span age, background, profession, and religion.

---

* 1997 – 2002 ©GlaxoSmithKline, citing American Podiatric
  Medical Association, www.apma.org.

The moderator delivered some opening remarks and asked everyone to spend a few minutes before lunch making introductions, revealing where we lived, what we did for work, and why we'd come to the event. As we went through the exercise, I spotted a large African-American gentleman seated across the table from me. During his turn, he introduced himself with a name that was clearly Muslim. Then, halfway through the program, he caught my eye across the table and, in the midst of bustling conversations and clinking silverware, mouthed the words, "I *love* your books!"

Reflexively, I swiveled my head around to see if perhaps a bona fide author had approached our table from behind. Finding no one there, I turned back, dumbfounded, pointed my finger toward my chest, and mouthed, "Me?"

Grinning, he said, "Yes! Let's talk after lunch."

Yeah — a dose of intrigue ran through my mind — *let's do that.*

The lunch progressed while I racked my brain, searching for a rational explanation for how this Muslim man had stumbled upon my distinctly Christian books.

Afterward, he waved me over and began fitting the puzzle pieces together. "I now understand that my comment was probably a little confusing because you assume I'm a Muslim," he said.

"I try *never* to assume anything in situations like these," I laughed, "but yeah, I'm a little curious."

As he related his story, my heart and mind awakened afresh to the power of personal evangelism. The insight God would give me after interacting with this man would shed new light for me on how the Holy Spirit moves in the lives of Christ-followers when they commit to staying in vibrant, dynamic fellowship with God.

After the encounter, I spent weeks thinking about his comments and growing increasingly awestruck by my discoveries about what *must* occur in the lives of Christ-followers for them to lead lives of impact.

• • • •

My tablemate had been a Muslim most of his life. He pointed out that being an African-American Muslim in a southern city, coupled with his current line of work, made for an often-uncomfortable existence.

"It hasn't been an easy go," he said. "As you might imagine, I've had a lot of struggles in social settings. And in my profession we have a lot of cocktail parties and other evening events. The natural pattern for me is to show up fashionably late, graciously accept a drink and something to eat, and throw my efforts into trying to make some business connections. Inevitably, I wind up standing alone, stuck against a wall or isolated in a corner. As soon as I think I've lasted as long as social etiquette requires, I discretely plot my exit and then leave. It's just something I've learned to live with.

"One night, I was at this type of party. As usual, I noticed several small circles of people forming to chat about this or that. I wasn't included, but again, I've become accustomed to the scenario.

"At one point, I saw a man on the other side of the room engrossed in discussion with a few people of his own kind, if you will. Suddenly he looked away from that particular group and noticed me standing alone by the far wall. This is exactly how it happened, Bill. He extricated himself from his conversational clique, walked clear across the room, stuck out his hand to me, and introduced himself.

"You know, it was so easy and so natural," the Muslim man continued. "In the moments that followed, we talked about our mutual profession, about our families and business and sports. Eventually our conversation found its way to issues of faith. I took a risk in telling him that I was Muslim —I was a little hesitant about how he'd respond. He told me he was a Christ-follower but that, truth be told, he knew almost nothing about Islam. You can imagine my surprise when he asked if I would do him the *courtesy* of explaining the basics of Islam over a cup of coffee sometime. Can you believe that? He said he was a curious type and genuinely wanted to understand my faith system and why I'd devoted my life to it.

"The next time we met, whatever doubts I had about him truly wanting to hear my beliefs were quickly dispelled. He *really* sought to understand my life and faith. We began meeting almost weekly, and each time I sat across from him, I was stunned by what an engaged and compassionate listener he was.

"One week, I even took the opportunity to ask him about his beliefs. I'd been a Christian as a kid but had left God, left the faith, left it all because the church my family attended was so racially prejudiced. I wanted no part of *that* Christianity. When the tables turned and I was on the receiving end of *his* faith story, he patiently described why he'd given his whole life to this person named Jesus Christ. I couldn't believe how easily the conversations evolved—and how respectfully and sensitively he conveyed his love of God. Despite our deep-seated religious differences, we were becoming fast friends.

"It went on this way for some time as we'd meet to hash through nuances of our faith experiences. Sometimes he would ask for a couple of days to find answers to my questions; other times, he knew exactly where I was struggling and seemed to have the perfect words to untangle my confusion. There finally came a day—I remember being home alone when this happened—that I felt totally compelled to pray to God. I kneeled beside my bed, told God everything I was feeling, and in the end gave my life to Jesus Christ. And in the space of about a week, that single decision changed *everything* in my world! Every single thing."

•   •   •   •   •

My heart was so full as his testimony washed over me. What a gripping story! I discovered that he'd recently become part of the leadership in his local church, which is where he had come across some of my books. And his steps of faith had already impacted his family, several of whom had begun making strides toward Christ. He really had begun a completely new life—one immersed in the companionship, power, and saving grace of Jesus Christ.

As I stood in the emptying ballroom of a sterile hotel on a muggy afternoon in the Deep South, I held my own private worship service, thanking God for redeeming this man, thanking God for changing his forever and for changing, very likely, the forevers of his immediate family.

All because of one person's walk across the room.

ENTERING THE ZONE
OF THE UNKNOWN

I must hear a dozen salvation stories a week while traveling and ministering on behalf of Willow Creek. They come in various forms from all sorts of men, women, and children, and I celebrate each and every one of them! But on that day, as I sat on the airplane flying me to the next city, an interesting thought raced through my mind, warranting special reflection: *What if redirecting a person's forever really is as simple as walking across a room?*

There was something about that story that God wanted to sear into me, and it dealt with far more than the end result of a man coming to faith in Christ. It was as if God himself said, "If you'll invest some energy thinking about this story, I'll give you an image that will fire you up for a long, long time."

And as I mulled it over, what came into focus was a clear picture of what things must have been like for the Christ-follower during that cocktail party. He'd found himself in a social setting, engaged in what I have always deemed to be a "circle of conversational comfort." He was involved with a group in which it was easy for him to relate and effortless for him to engage. There was zero threat of anything risky or unsafe unfolding, which is why he had every reason to stay within the boundaries of that little Circle of Comfort, a place we've all enjoyed on one occasion or another.

Yet drawn by the fact that one man stood unintentionally and uncomfortably alone, he left that circle and walked stride by stride across the room. It was as though in a flash of insight, he heard a word of encouragement directly from the Holy Spirit: "Why don't you go over and extend a hand of friendship to that guy? Go see if he may need a little conversation or encouragement—who knows what might happen?"

As I chewed on the thought, I realized that not only did he see something and hear something as the Spirit guided him; he also *felt* something worthy of acting upon. The Spirit living inside him caused him to feel such compassion for the man standing alone that he excused himself from his Circle of Comfort, made the turn to the other side of the room, and started walking in the direction of a place I call the "Zone of the Unknown."

It's foreign territory, this zone. He had no clue what would happen when he stuck out his hand to the tall Muslim man. He knew nothing about where the conversation would go or if there would be any conversation at all. He was uncertain what this individual's reaction to him would be. But he was already committed. He had left his Circle of Comfort, he had walked by faith all the way across the room, and he had resolved in his heart, probably praying every step of the way, to enter into the Zone of the Unknown and see what God might do. (In my opinion, it's within this zone that God does his very *best* work.)

I couldn't think of another life-change story that had had as much impact on me. *But why?* I kept pestering God. *What is it about this one?*

The power of it, I concluded, was that it gave me a framework for something I'd been thinking about since my own salvation experience more than thirty years earlier: personal evangelism really *can* be as simple as a walk across a room—just a few ordinary Spirit-guided steps can have truly extraordinary outcomes.

CHRIST'S WALK ACROSS THE ROOM

There was an intriguing subplot to what God was revealing. It's as if he were saying to me, "*Now* you grasp with a fresh grip what my Son did."

Track with me along metaphorical lines, and I think you'll agree that the original (and consummate) work of personal evangelism began with a walk across a "room"—a very large room, in fact. At a certain point in history, Jesus Christ himself left the marvelous fellowship of the Trinity and the worship and adoration of the angels; he wrapped himself in human flesh, and he walked across the cosmos in order to stretch out a hand to people like you and me—many of whom were right in the middle of wrecking their lives.

Romans 5:8 summarizes Christ's redemptive strides: it was when we were helplessly in the throes of sin that Christ extracted himself from the *ultimate* Circle of Comfort—heaven itself—to step across time and space to rescue us. Jesus took a decided step toward the ungodly, embracing the worst this planet had to offer with acceptance and love and forgiveness. Miraculously, Christ's death for rebellious and sin-scarred people declared amnesty for *everyone*.

Think about it: giving your life for a noble person is one thing, but laying it all down for vagrants like us? It was an undeserved and unexpected move, to say the least. And the correlation is revolutionary to Christ-followers: we take walks across rooms because *he* took the ultimate walk across a room.

If you've ever wondered why God would go to such lengths to prove his love, you're in good company. To clear up any confusion his first-century audience might have had about why he came, Christ said, "I came to seek and to save what was lost."

That's it. *People* were Jesus' One Thing. And they still are. People who are sick. People who are lonely. People who are wandering, depressed, and hopeless. People who have gotten themselves tangled up in suffocating habits and destructive relationships.

I think of the story from John 8 when Christ appears in the temple courts, all set to teach the crowd that has gathered there. A group of Pharisees arrive on the scene, dragging with them a woman with a checkered moral past who's just been caught in the act of adultery. Imagine the horror of being thrust into such a public place, your worst sins on display for the masses to see. Adultery is a serious offense, the Pharisees argue, and in keeping with

God's Law from the days of Moses, Jesus will surely agree to have this woman stoned to death because of her ghastly sin.

The Pharisees know that Jesus is in a bind, and you sense from the text that they enjoy, with a sort of morbid delight, forcing the self-proclaimed Messiah into the middle of a moral dilemma: If he lets the woman off the hook, he'll be denying the validity of the law. But if he allows her to be stoned, he might be accused of being unmerciful — or even of being an enemy of the Roman government, which was the only group allowed to carry out capital punishment.

Jesus' reaction is fascinating. "I assume you're going to stone her," he begins. "So if that's true, then let's at least bring some order to the process. Go ahead and stone her, but let's just form a line, and those of you with *no* sin, you get to be at the front of the line. You throw your rocks first."

Obviously, Christ's plan wrecks the Pharisees' whole day. And understandably, the law-loving Pharisees have no reply. One by one, their rocks thump to the sand and they walk away.

Jesus finds himself alone with this woman who has tasted forgiveness and mercy for the first time. Although he has every right to get in her face and criticize her poor life choices, the Bible says he chooses a different course. His travel-weary knees softly creak as he crouches down beside her, his eyes wet with tears. "I don't condemn you — really. That's not why I came. I came to redeem your failures, not to punish you for your mistakes. Now go—don't sin anymore. Start living a brand-new life today! Don't fall back into your same sinful habits. I will help you live a new life starting right here, right now."

Is there a better picture of God's heart than this—the heart that invites someone to freedom instead of indictment? Without excusing the woman's sinful indiscretions, Jesus said, "Everyone has taken some wrong turns. Everyone is in need of forgiveness and redemption and healing. Everyone needs to know the love that only my Father can provide. *That* is why I've come." And with customary tenacity, he left the temple courts that day, unwavering in his belief that his restorative vision would one day be reality.

Still today, as you love people, serve people, point people toward faith in Christ, redirect wayward people, restore broken people, and develop people into the peak of their spiritual potential, you reaffirm your understanding of your primary mission in the world.

TUNING IN TO HEAVEN

Several years ago, I was copiloting a private aircraft that was headed back to Chicago from the West Coast. Piloting the plane was a gentleman I'd flown with several times before. On each occasion, once we reached cruising altitude and switched on the autopilot, we'd enjoy open conversations about any number of issues.

On that particular night, our dialogue was generally about the task at hand. We discussed flight patterns and weather conditions and altitude assessments, mostly prompted by air traffic controllers on the ground who were feeding updates to us. But with about ninety minutes left in the flight, I silently pleaded for God's intervention. *Help me direct things to more substantive issues.*

After the next intercom update, I ventured into the Zone of the Unknown and asked my pilot friend if he would ever make a flight like this without listening to air traffic control. Would he ever consider—even for a moment—silencing the radio and directing the flight alone?

He didn't waste any time answering. "Of course not!" he laughed. "It'd be crazy—I need all the information and assistance I can get my hands on ... especially in dicey weather."

I prayed for a boost of confidence and then said, "If you can believe it, some people fly through their entire life with the radio to heaven turned off. They receive zero input from God. They get no guidance, no wisdom, and no counsel. A lot of times, they fly blindly into bad weather and end up crashing and burning. You'd be surprised how many people do that."

Silence crept through the cockpit as I waited and prayed.

A few seconds later, his voice now sobered, he said, "I guess that would be pretty stupid, wouldn't it?"

I conceded that there were probably better approaches to life and then sat there awestruck as a full hour of redemptive dialogue unfolded en route to Chicago. "Well, how do you turn the 'radio' on?" he had asked. And so, in the most straightforward language I could find, I told him.

* * * * *

Several days later, I reflected on the boldness I'd exhibited during that flight. I haven't always been so daring, but as I gave it some thought, I landed on an explanation for why it seemed to be showing up more often: I *really* believe the saving message of Jesus Christ. I don't only preach it; I believe it! I honestly believe that every wayward person I know would live a vastly better life if God's love, grace, and redemption were operating in their lives.

Do you believe this too? A man once told me that he never shares his faith with anyone. I thought it was an interesting comment and probed a little as to why he was so resolved about his role (or lack thereof) in evangelism.

His answer shocked me. "I would never want to inflict the burden of God on anyone," he said.

Wow. That is not at all the God I know, I thought. The God I know invaded my world with love, acceptance, and grace and stuck me on the back of a launched rocket at age seventeen that I still haven't peeled myself off of. Nor do I want to anytime soon!

But it's an interesting thought to ponder, isn't it: *Who is the God you know?*

Is the God you know full of grace and mercy and compassion? Is the God you know mysterious, surprising, captivating? Is he forever unchanging and yet always brand new? Does he inspire you with his big ideas about how your life can really count? Is he faithful?

In my experience, the people who find themselves taking walks across rooms have first landed on the belief that the God they know is *worth* knowing! They have cultivated a heart posture that says, "Well, of course everyone I know would want this type of relationship with God! I'm absolutely sure you'd all love what I'm experiencing here…."

If you are in love with the God you know, let me ask you to rewind your faith journey a little to your pre-Christian days. Recall that time in your life when you would get up in the morning and realize once again that you had nobody to share your day with. *Guess I'm doing this one alone too*, you'd think. Or you would drive to work and be the only one in your car. You'd have long stretches of time with no words from heaven and nothing supernatural invading your ho-hum world. You would violate your conscience and have zero awareness that grace could actually cover it, if only you'd ask.

My friend, if you have been wrecked by God's gift of new life—as I thankfully have—and if you want to live your life as an expression of love for the great God you know, then let's crank up our boldness meters and introduce as many people as possible to the God who wants desperately to enfold them in his grace!

THE GREATEST GIFT

My belief system hasn't always been so firm, but when I was in my early twenties and a student at Trinity College, my professor Dr. Gilbert Bilezikian delivered lessons that inspired me, convicted me, and compelled me to action. To a group of us who were leading a high school ministry at the time, Dr. B said, "Throughout the course of your life, you're going to give your life to something. You will. *All* people do. They give their lives to pleasure or to possessions, to the attainment of popularity or to the acquisition of more power. But always to something."

As he plowed ahead, I got sidelined by my own questions. What was I giving my life to? What was the one great *something* I was living for? I began to wonder whether I was really as concerned about other people as I said I was or if I was just hiding my self-interest behind a facade of interest. My heart shuddered as I stared at the truth about what captivated most of my thoughts. It wasn't exactly laudable.

During that season of life, I had been anticipating a lucrative career in business. But as Dr. B's words crept deeper into my heart, I was suddenly and powerfully drawn to one prevailing preoccupation—people. People who face a Christless eternity. People who are ostracized and isolated and hopeless. People who are living for achievements that do not fulfill, accolades that never satisfy, and money that doesn't bring genuine happiness.

I wanted to approach life like Jesus had. The mind of Christ hadn't been consumed by business gains or money or fame but instead was endlessly focused on one thing: people—those who were lost and found, young and old, rich and poor, sought-after and rejected. Never has anyone displayed such a prodigious obsession with people as did Jesus. And in his customarily straightforward style, Dr. B reminded me that Jesus' expectation is that his followers *share* this magnificent obsession.

"True followers of Christ who really get it right," he said, "give themselves to *people*. Most importantly, they give themselves to pointing people to faith in Christ. That is the highest and best use of a human life—to have it serve as a signpost that points people toward God." Dr. B summed up my entire belief system with a brilliant flash of insight: if you really believe in the redeeming and transforming power of God's presence in a person's life, then the single greatest gift you can give someone is an explanation of how to be rightly connected to him.

It's as though Jesus is saying to his followers, "What I did as I walked across the cosmos all those years ago, I now want *you* to do. Every day, try to point every person you meet to me. Live as though you actually *believe* that your parent, your coworker, and your neighbor would be better off if they knew my Father—if they were on the receiving end of his counsel, his wisdom, and his guidance. Become walk-across-the-room people who follow my lead! Be people who are willing to seize every opportunity I give you—not motivated by guilt or fear or obligation, but just with an eye on me, a pliable heart, and a passion for my people."

These days, I recognize just how correct Dr. B was. Because when most people I talk to really think through their own faith journeys, they land on the fact that Christ wasn't the only one who took a walk to rescue them. Almost without exception, Christ-followers tell me that their faith stories involve someone somewhere who took a risk to walk across a room and to reflect the curiosity, kindness, and love of Christ. Someone somewhere made the decision to take the gift they'd been given and bestow it on them—at the time, a wayward soul living very far from God.

When you choose to live by faith instead of by sight, taking these walks, extending yourself, and exhibiting care to people who need to be enfolded in community, there is something a lot like Jesus going on in your mind and spirit. According to the apostle Paul, it was Jesus who, "being in the very nature God, did not consider equality with God something to be used to his advantage; rather, he made himself nothing by taking the very nature of a servant, being made in human likeness. And being found in appearance as a human being, he humbled himself by becoming obedient to death—even death on a cross!"*

Let me say it again: the single greatest gift you can give someone is an introduction to the God who asked his Son to go the unthinkable distance to redeem them. And when you allow your life's great preoccupation to be people, you'll find that when Christ asks you to take a walk across a street, into a restaurant, up a flight of stairs, through a locker room, wherever, you are ready! You're ready to leave your Circle of Comfort and follow his lead because you remember the fact that Jesus once crossed an entire universe to rescue you—the same Jesus who was known to enjoy deep community from time to time but who would consistently and unapologetically excuse himself from a Circle of Comfort and

---

* Philippians 2:6–8.

walk in the direction of someone he could direct toward the Father.

Today, to Christ-followers all over the planet, he says, "Reflect my love! And repeat my action."

TAKE A WALK!

When my son was in the fifth or sixth grade, he joined a soccer league. And although Todd was a talented athlete for his age, team sports were a little intimidating to him.

The man who served for the next three years as Todd's soccer coach was a businessman named Brian, a fantastic guy who really loved kids. Miraculously, he built hope and confidence into my otherwise-apprehensive son and actually sold Todd on the idea that he could be a terrific soccer player.

For three years I stood on the sidelines at almost every game. My wife, Lynne, my daughter, Shauna, and I cheered for Todd beside other parents who were rooting for their little guys, all of us engaging in the obnoxious hollering that families do at youth soccer matches. Afterward, we'd typically enjoy a few minutes of fellowship with other families that attended Willow.

One afternoon, Brian was in the center of the field after a long day, loading cones into his car so that he could head home. Just then, the Holy Spirit said, "Walk across the soccer field and help him, Hybels.

Leave this safe little group, and go see if you can get to know Brian." I can replay the scene in my mind as if it happened yesterday.

As I put one foot in front of the other and headed toward where Brian stood, I tried to prepare myself for whatever might unfold once I opened my mouth. *Ought to be interesting,* I thought.

After introducing myself, we chatted about the kids on the team, about what line of work Brian was involved in, and eventually about my occupation. He wasn't too thrilled to discover that I was a pastor, but as weeks went by, he continued to engage in brief conversations with me after games or practices.

Each time we talked, I would thank Brian for the meaningful impact he was having on my son. "I appreciate how much time you volunteer out of your busy schedule to coach these kids," I would tell him. "I think what you are doing is noble and classy, Brian. I'll always be grateful."

On one day in particular, when we were nearing a holiday service at Willow, I was prompted by the Spirit to walk across that soccer field again, this time to see if Brian would like to attend the service. Mustering an additional ounce of courage with each step I took, I asked him if he would consider coming to Willow just once with me.

His response instantly erased any hope of receptivity on his part. "Oh, man, Bill, I *knew* it would turn into this! I just *knew* someday it would land here. Look, I know plenty about Willow Creek—I get tied up in its traffic every week. The whole thing frustrates me. God is not part of my life, church is not part of my life, and I'd just as soon take this whole thing off of the agenda here." (Hey, at least he was clear.)

"Okay, Brian," I said, trying to relax him. "No pressure, I promise. I'm committed to respecting your wishes."

And each week the following year, I would walk step by step across that soccer field to help him pick up balls and cones. How small those steps felt! Was I helping at all?

"How'd things go this week?" I'd ask. And we would talk about business and the deals he was working on. Then he would ask me how my week had been. I suppose my no-pressure approach served its purpose: I no longer offended Brian with unsolicited invitations to church. But to me, the whole experience seemed like an exercise in spiritual water-treading.

Eventually Todd cycled out of the soccer league, and I lost contact with Brian altogether. Frankly, I assumed I'd never see him again. But after several years had passed, the day came when Brian's world was turned dramatically upside down. Business issues shifted. His family life tilted. In sobering and unexpected ways, pain and despair walked through

the front door of his life and took up residence
there.

He picked up the phone and called me one afternoon to ask if he could come by to talk. "I *don't* want
to come to a service," he clarified. "I just need to talk
about a few things."

After that initial meeting in my office, Brian and
I would meet several times, but I'd sense only minuscule progress during the conversations. At some
point, he stopped calling altogether. And although I
wondered how he was managing in life and whether
or not he'd ironed out his pain, I honored his desire
to lead the pace of our relationship.

Months later, I was standing at the front of the
auditorium preparing a group of new believers for
their upcoming baptism experience. As I explained
the meaning, purpose, and significance of water baptism, I looked to my left and saw Brian sitting there,
right in the front row. *He has no idea where he is!* I
thought. *He's in a baptism meeting, for crying out loud.
How did he stumble into this one?* I regained my com-
posure long enough to finish my comments, being
extraordinarily careful to complete my instructions
in a way that wouldn't screen out a guy like Brian for
the rest of his life. There was no way he was ready for
the *baptism* deal!

After the meeting, I approached Brian and asked
him to walk with me to the parking lot. "I've got to
get going," I explained, "but let's at least talk on the

way out." As soon as we had moved away from the crowds, I stopped and looked Brian right in the eyes. "What in the world were you doing in a baptism meeting?"

His answer floored me.

"A couple of months ago, I snuck in during a service and sat in the back. You were giving a message on abandoning the self-improvement plan and getting on board with the grace plan instead. You talked about the need to open ourselves to God by accepting the work of his Son, Jesus Christ. And on that day, Bill, I gave my heart to Christ. So what I'm saying is, I was here tonight — believe it or not — because I want to be *baptized*."

His face was beaming as mine fell slack-jawed. I couldn't hide my astonishment. "You have *got* to be kidding me. Really. You have got to be kidding me!" I stood there staring at him with a dumbfounded look on my face for probably two full minutes.

Sometime after that conversation, I had the privilege of baptizing Brian at Willow Creek, the place where he still continues to serve, the place where he fell in love with a godly woman and was married, and the place where he and his wife now teach other couples how to experience the joy and elation of a Christ-centered marriage.

A few weeks before Christmas a couple of years ago, I was headed to my office with Todd, who was all grown up by then. We turned the corner in a stairwell, careening right into a large, muscular man. Instinctively, I took a step back as I looked up. It was Brian! And in a split second, a fifteen-year void between my son and his favorite childhood coach was filled. With the type of love that only Christ-followers can manifest, he threw his arms around Todd's neck. "How great it is to see you!" Brian raved.

After a few moments of conversation, Brian headed down the steps. When he reached the first landing, he stopped and looked up at us. "Hey, Bill," he said, "I just want to thank you for all those times you walked across the soccer field and opened yourself up. Really ... thanks." And with that, he turned to go.

Friends, that's as good as it gets in my world. And my guess is that similar experiences would qualify for your life's as-good-as-it-gets moments too. Knowing that the God of the universe has equipped you to bestow the greatest gift in this life on another human being, choose today to lead a life of impact — eternal impact.

Take a walk! See what he might do.

CHAPTER 2

Develop Friendships

* * * * *

Recently, the management team at Willow convened for an all-day session in downtown Chicago to map out plans for a new neighborhood evangelism strategy. Our suburban neighborhoods were seeing hundreds of new rooftops appear, and we realized we needed to better equip our members for introducing a God-ward element into their relationships with people who live down the street, around the corner, or right next door. The goal was simple: come up with a way to enfold friends and neighbors in Chicagoland with the love of Christ—and do so *naturally.*

Our executive pastor stood at a flip chart, fat marker in hand, prompting us to distill our thoughts to the fundamental idea—the nut—of what we were really talking about. A few minutes into our discussion, one of my colleagues had a revelation unfold. "Isn't this ... isn't the whole *thing* about seeing how many neighbors we can take to heaven with us? Can't we boil it down to looking at people who live within a bike ride of our houses, and seeing how many of them we can take to heaven with us through the work of Christ?"

Everyone looked around the room as heads started to bob and energy began to rise. "Yeah. It doesn't have to be more complicated than that, does it?"

Think of it: when you got up today, whether you walked into an office complex, a construction site, an office, a classroom, the local grocery store, you were probably surrounded by a sea of faces—some belonging to friends you know and family members you treasure, others belonging to perfect strangers. Just imagine the shift in your focus if you made a habit of approaching *all* of them with this attitude: *My ultimate goal is to see how many of these people I can have on each elbow when I cross the finish line of this earthly life and run into God's presence for all of eternity!*

We immediately assigned one of our senior staff members, Garry Poole, to the role of testing out ways to achieve this goal in a few nearby neighborhoods. Soon Garry identified three distinct concepts that must be present to have maximum impact in our communities. Eventually, we coined the entire approach "Living in 3D." When effective walk-across-the-room people interact with others in their world, they

> Develop friendships—by engaging in the lives of people around them
>
> Discover stories—before sharing their own story and God's redemptive story
>
> Discern next steps—by following the Holy Spirit's direction

Most Christ-followers agree with these ideas. If you ask a hundred believers whether they have friends or family members who are living far from God and who face a Christless eternity, they will all say yes.

And if you ask the same group if they agree that our goal is to walk into heaven with as many of those people as possible by building relationships, understanding where they are in their faith journeys, and seizing opportunities to tell the story of God's love for them, again, most will agree.

But sit that group of a hundred down, look them directly in the eyes, and ask whether they are actively *doing the work* of telling their lost friends and family members about how to have a relationship with God. What do you think they'll say? It's conjecture, but based on my experience, you'll be lucky to find half of them engaged in the process. In short, Christ-followers don't disagree with the need for people to be pointed toward God. They just struggle with how to get it done.

CAN YOU SEE IT?

Over the Christmas break one year, my family and I accepted an invitation to a holiday party while on vacation. A friend who would be attending the same party tipped me off about an older businessman who had been vacationing in the same community for years. "I'm sure he'll be at the party," this friend began. "Look, just be aware that he's been through a divorce, and he's living with a woman now who's not his wife. He's into drinking … a lot of drinking. And … well, he *knows* who you are. He won't be too thrilled to bump into you at a party, you know, in a social setting like this. I wanted you to be fore-warned, that's all."

I walked away from that conversation thinking, *Give me a real challenge!* Or more the case, *Give God a real challenge!* I'd seen my fair share of crass, bra-zen men become tenderhearted once the Holy Spirit supernaturally intervened. I had stood there utterly amazed on many occasions as former druggies and adulterers and atheists softened to discussions of a spiritual nature. And each time, my belief was renewed that the Holy Spirit can accomplish outright miracles when Christ-followers stick their necks out in conveying the hope of the gospel.

That evening, my family and I arrived at the host couple's home as planned. As I headed into the living room, I literally ran into a gentleman who fit the gen-eral description of the businessman my friend had warned me about. Recovering, I stuck out my hand and said, "Hi, my name's Bill." He recognized who I was and sort of grunted as if to say, "Yeah, yeah, save it, buddy."

"We're kind of starting cold here, aren't we?" I laughed. He told me his name, confirming that this was in fact the guy I was supposed to avoid offending that evening. *He* would *be the first person I run into,* I thought.

Fumbling for some reasonable way to redeem our bumpy start, I asked him how long he'd been vacationing there and why he had chosen this particular spot over other places. Somewhere in his response, he mentioned that he loved the warmer climates and that he had been a boater for nearly four decades.

"What a coincidence! I love boating!" I blurted out. I cautioned him that if we started down the boat path, he'd never get me to shut up.

"Do you have a boat?" he said, as if shocked to discover that I was human. I began explaining the whole thing, the words tumbling out of my mouth—how I had fallen headlong into a love affair with boating and sailboat racing, what kinds of boats I'd sailed, my favorite waters, the fact that my son, only twenty-three at the time, had recently sailed solo from South Haven, Michigan, all through the Great Lakes, out the New York barge canal, all the way down to Florida, and eventually throughout most of the Bahamas island chain. "Here! Meet my son, Todd!" I said as I prodded Todd toward the man.

"You're *both* boaters!" he exclaimed. "How about that!" As we continued chatting, I could tell his preconceived ideas about me were dissipating into thin air. By this time, he was anxious to keep talking—to me an indication of the open door I'd hoped for.

"So how did you get down here?" he asked.

I explained that my family had flown down commercially this time, which somehow led to him telling me all about the private plane that he always brought to this particular location. Stunned, I said, "You have a plane? How about that! I got my pilot's license when I was sixteen."

"Me too!" he laughed. "What are the chances? Same age and everything. What kind of ratings do you have?"

We talked planes for the next twenty minutes, and once that conversation exhausted itself, we started down the what-you-do-for-a-living path. It turned out that the one and only person I knew who worked in the same industry as this man was a good friend of his. "I can't believe you know him!" he nearly shouted. And silently I thought, *Of course I know him. How typical of God!*

Of *course* God put this man right by the door as I entered the party. Of *course* God saw to it that there were common denominators for us to discover. Of *course* God gave me a few hints about what to say, how to respond, and how to listen well. Of *course* God allowed for a bridge to be built there, instead of deepening the cliché chasm that says the "God guy" and the "pagan guy" just can't relate.

After we got over the initial shock of sharing a mutual acquaintance, I said, "Well, here's one you'll enjoy. Less than a week ago, your good friend came to a party in my home after attending a Christmas Eve service at our church."

The guy's voice was drenched with disbelief. "He *never* goes to church," he said. "I *know* he never goes to church."

"Well, he came to church and actually said he loved it," I said, which elicited a "No *way!*" from the businessman. We had a good laugh and then went our separate ways to mingle with others at the party, continuing the conversation periodically throughout the night. Each time I'd spot him from across the room, I'd have a good chuckle with God. *I can just see it, God*, I'd think. *I can see exactly what this guy will be like once you rock his world!*

At the end of the evening in a clandestine gesture, he slid a business card in my hand. "The next time you're in Chicago and I'm in Chicago," he said, "I might buy you dinner. And who knows, you may be able to drag me to that church of yours."

◦   ◦   ◦   •

As he walked out the door that night, I thought about all of the dynamics at work in how that whole deal unfolded. He had been forewarned that I would be there, and in his mind I had a huge target on my forehead from the moment I entered the house. If I had played my "God card" immediately—telling him how I loved being a Christian and how he should become one too—things would have headed south in a heartbeat.

Instead, I just focused on developing a friendship with him, telling him about things that I truly enjoy in addition to God. I have lots of meaningful pursuits in life that center on God and his redemptive kingdom agenda. But I also have passionate interest in other things, two of which are boating and flying. And I feel enormous freedom to talk about interests I love, both regarding God and regarding things other than God.

I hope that as you engage in the world around you, you'll go for broke in your interactions with people, starting with the ones right in front of you. Be the one who catches the vision for how the man or woman standing in front of you will look once God's redeeming power does its work in his or her life.

CHAPTER 3

Discover Stories

· · · · ·

After what had been a long day of back-to-back meetings in downtown Chicago one Tuesday night, I opted to stay inside the Loop until rush hour had passed. I'd promised a friend that I would review his book manuscript, and knowing the traffic would be a bear for a couple of hours, I decided to find a place where I could get some work done before making the drive back to the suburbs.

I walked into the restaurant of a nice hotel. There was a crowded lounge on one side and a busy dining room on the other. As I stood there trying to decide which side would be more conducive to my working, a young couple entered through the main door. They walked up next to me and engaged in their own deliberation about where they should sit. They were chatting and laughing, appearing open to whatever might happen, so I made eye contact with them. "Hey, I've never eaten here," I ventured. "Would you suggest the lounge or the dining room?"

"We've never eaten here either, and we were going to ask you the same thing!"

They both had easygoing smiles and seemed friendly enough. We exchanged first names, and they

asked me if I was waiting on someone or if I was
there alone. They'd flown in earlier from out of town
and were completely unfamiliar with the area. Since
I'd been to their city on several occasions, we were off
to the races conversationally. We talked about local
attractions in their area, what's interesting to do in
Chicago, mutually favorite travel destinations, you
name it.

The man excused himself after a few minutes to
check in at the host stand. When he returned, he
offered to get us all something to drink. He said it
could be awhile before a table was ready in either
room, but why didn't we take a seat at the bar while
we waited. Although I thought that sounded like a
grand idea, I realized I was probably intruding on a
quiet night out for them. "Listen, I'm fine being alone
if I'm throwing a wrench in your date," I said.

Have you ever had one of those experiences where
people laugh a little too energetically in response to
a not-so-funny comment? I registered their reaction
for future reference. "Sure, then," I recovered. "Let's
grab a drink."

For the next half hour, we covered a half dozen
topics—their backgrounds, my wife and kids, rec-
reational passions, and more. It was a ball! I thought
it interesting that they never asked me what I did for
a living, but I would soon discover that maybe that
was for the best.

At one point the woman looked at me, serious now, and said, "Bill, it sounds like you're a pretty happy man." She said it with incredible genuineness and tenderness. Just then, I felt the tug of the Holy Spirit—viscerally I could feel it. *Here's an open door,* he was nudging. *Just walk through it. You've already walked across this restaurant, you've engaged this couple in conversation, you're open, and I'm asking you to walk through this door. Just test the waters to see if they might be ready to talk about something deeper than sports teams and travel destinations.*

In the brief time I'd been with this couple, my heart had expanded toward them. I wondered how life really was for them and whether or not they were fulfilled. I was curious about where they were spiritually and if they were involved in a church somewhere. I had no idea where this conversation was headed, but I secretly hoped I'd be able to say a word for God.

And so I took another small risk. "You know," I said, without any hype or syrup, "I'm one of the happiest people I know. I have a great life. I love what I do and the people I do it with. I'm blessed with a terrific family and friends. I'm healthy, I'm optimistic about the future. All in all, I'm a happy camper."

They seemed to be open still. "How about you?" I ventured. "Where does your happiness meter read these days?" I asked the question playfully enough that had they wanted to bail on the conversation, they could have.

The woman didn't hesitate, though her voice was suddenly shaky. "Actually, my meter's reading pretty low at the moment. Our company just laid off three of my closest friends, and it's been a tough go. We've all worked together for a long time.... I guess I'm taking things pretty hard."

The man then said that he'd been in an all-day meeting to determine how many more staff people he had to cut in his situation. "It's a painful time for our industry right now, and the turmoil of letting good people go is awful." We talked about what it's like to lose friends to layoffs, and I was deeply moved by their immense concern for their colleagues.

"I'm touched by your care for the people you work with. I just wonder how the two of you are handling all of this," I said. "I mean, it seems like you both have a lot of pressure in your careers. How does it affect your relationship?"

Things got very quiet. Too quiet. They paused a moment too long, and I took my cue. "Look, I'm sorry if this is too heavy for your night out. We can go back to talking beaches, vacations, all that...."

They looked at each other for a second, seeming to strike a nonverbal agreement to "just tell me" something. In my mind, I geared up to absorb details about the enormous marital strife their work stress had caused for them.

Was I ever wrong.

"You should probably know that we're not married," the woman began. I checked my reflexes and realized I hadn't reacted yet. Thankfully, I still appeared to be holding steady as a nonjudging listener.

"We're just good friends. Well, actually," she continued, "we're both gay."

Now, I don't know what you say when someone tells you something like that. But here's one thing I do know: your immediate reaction is going to make or break you. Regardless of how much trust you've forged to that point, if your *initial* response isn't filled with acceptance and compassion, I guarantee you're done. So, despite the fact that her statement had totally blindsided me, I knew I had to foster an elastic framework with this couple. I had to land on some sort of paradigm that could bend and flex to include them too. But how?

Although the entire conversation had moved so quickly to that point, now it was as if life was unfolding in slow motion. While they waited for me to respond, God and I had a quick chat. More the case, I suppose, I shamelessly begged him for help.

911! I screamed in my spirit. *I could use some help down here! You got me into this, and if you tell me that I'm third in line right now to receive an answer from you, I'm here to tell you that that's not good enough! I need some direction, God, and I need it pronto!*

I felt completely ambushed as hyperactive thoughts flooded my mind. Before I could organize them all, a few words fell out of my mouth: "Well, if you want to talk about *that*, we'd better get another round of drinks! This time, on me."

Just then, the host stopped by to tell us a lounge table was available, and to my astonishment, they agreed to continue the conversation there. I will remember the next sixty minutes we spent around that table for a long, long time. It was incredible — divine, even. They obviously needed to open up to someone, and I happened to be in the right place at the right time.

Their pain level was high in so many areas, and as they continued to talk, I thanked God for orchestrating our meeting. They described the painful treatment they received from people they cared deeply about. They elaborated on the sense of isolation they felt at work — knowing coworkers steered clear of them once they discovered the homosexual lifestyle these two were leading.

My mind trailed off as I wondered how they would respond if and when they learned that I was a pastor of a church. As I reengaged in the flow of conversation, I caught the man's eyes for a brief moment and was jolted by how cold and steely they now seemed.

"You know things are bad when your dad won't even talk to you," he said, moving away from the work situation. "And when he does communicate, it's only through the mail. He's a really religious guy, and he writes me letters to tell me what an abomination I am before God and that I'm headed to hell in a handbasket. That's about all he says to me."

That comment prompted my second 911 plea to God. Now I *knew* the stakes were high, and I was staggered by the implications of him finding out I was a "religious type" too. I did *not* want to botch this.

I silently replayed his comments about his dad calling him an abomination and condemning him to hell in a handbasket. *Please, God*, I thought, *please give me some direction and discernment here.* I knew all of the wrong things I could say in this situation, but unfortunately, the right ones eluded me.

How did I get myself into this, anyway? I needed time to think and space to assess how to reengage with compassion and conviction. As soon as he finished his sentence, as if on autopilot, this is what I heard myself say: "Well, I'm probably more religious than you think. But the people who teach me about God say that he has an unconditional sort of love for people of any color, any background, who are fighting any kind of difficulty. What I'm taught is that there is a God who feels *outrageous* compassion for every single person, regardless of their situation. And two words that I carry around with me to remember these things every day are *grace* and *power*. They're significant to me.

"I walk through each day believing that God's grace can cover my shortcomings—and trust me, I have a lot of shortcomings. I also believe that God's power can help me face any challenge that confronts me."

The man looked at me and said, "The only two God-words that float around in my head are *judgment* and *hell*."

My suggestion came slowly. "Why don't you just trade them out?"

The guy sort of chuckled. "Just swap them out? I mean … can you *do* that?"

"Yep. Just swap them out for a week or two and see what happens," I said. "Look, every time you think *judgment* and *hell*, give yourself an opportunity to think about God differently and just say the words *grace* and *power*. You never know what might unfold."

The woman then looked at him and said, "Guess it couldn't hurt."

Her words hung in the air unchallenged, and mysteriously, the mood supernaturally lightened. Someone walked by and bumped our chairs. Something caught our attention and caused us to laugh. Real life pierced our conversational bubble once again, and I realized for the first time that we had savored nearly an hour of uninterrupted dialogue at that little table.

The host approached us again to ask if we wanted to relocate to a table that had just opened up in the dining room, but knowing how weary they were and the hour's drive I faced, we all agreed to call it a night.

As we gathered our coats and made our way to the door, the woman turned to me and said, "Tonight was extraordinary. Really, you have no idea." She wrapped her arms around me to embrace me. Despite my well-known aversion to hugs, even I appreciated the gesture.

The man shook my hand slowly and said, "Thank you so much for talking to us tonight. Let's see, what were those two words again?"

"*Grace* and *power*," I said. "*Grace* and *power.*"

"Yeah, *grace* and *power*," he said. "I'll give it a try this week." And with that, they climbed into a cab and left.

·   ·   ·   ·   •

Now, before you mull over that story, let me be clear about a few things. At no point during the evening did this couple fall on their knees in submission to Jesus Christ. In fact, I never really had the chance to share the plan of salvation. I didn't invite them to attend Willow, nor did we exchange business cards, because I don't carry them. In fact, it is doubtful I will see this couple again this side of eternity. As far as I know, that evening was my one and only shot. (I tried to silence old tapes from my younger "evange-lism training" days—you could probably guess the question that floated through my mind: "But what if their cab gets hit by a garbage truck ten minutes from now?!")

That being said, if we agree that the goal is to somehow introduce people to the God who created them, who loves them, and who longs to save them, then how do you think I did that night? If living in 3D means developing friendships and discovering the other person's story before launching into an unsolicited telling of the plan of salvation, I pray I honored God that night.

CHAPTER 4

Discern Next Steps

During a Super Bowl party a few years ago, I got into an interesting conversation with a gentleman I'd never met before. Just as the halftime show was ending, he started opening up about some deep issues. I got the sense that something supernatural was happening, but as the room began to buzz again with excitement for the second half, everyone's attention was refocused on the giant screen in front of us. It wasn't exactly an opportune time to pull him off to the side and start in on the Sinner's Prayer.

I took inventory of my motivations, realizing that all I really wanted to do was serve him. I didn't have lofty notions of being the one to help him cross the line of faith right then and there. Nor was I expecting an offer from him to skip the second half and hole away so that we could hash through the essential doctrines of Christianity. I knew he wanted to see the game, as did I, but I also knew our interaction was not accidental.

Before we rejoined the crowd, I asked if there was any way I could serve him in his spiritual quest—anything he could think of that I might do to help.

His answer was heartfelt. "If you wouldn't mind, pray that I'd be able to understand this faith thing more."

"Of course," I agreed. "And if anything else comes to mind, I hope you'll let me know."

He then admitted that he'd never read a "Christian" book but said that if I'd send him something, he'd read *one* chapter. "But only one!" he added. The good-natured grin on his face told me that his restriction was only half-serious, but I took him up on the challenge.

As soon as I returned home, I stared at the book spines on my library shelves, trying to figure out which book to send, knowing I had only a single chapter to work with. One shot!

I prayed as I scanned the shelves, my adrenaline pumping. *Father, direct me to the right book. Take my preferences out of the equation altogether.... This is all about him. Just show me what it is that you want him to read. Lead me to the right book, and I'll make sure he receives it.*

THE THIRD *D*

If you want to become a walk-across-the-room person, then you will choose to Develop friendships with people in your world and then take risks to Discover their stories. Now on to the third D—discerning next step.

Next steps are the ones that follow those steps that took you across the room in the first place. The ones that tend to be risky, but in a calculated sort of way—because the Spirit is guiding. So although Christ-followers never know exactly how next steps will be received, they continue to risk testing a few, acknowledging that spiritual ground will never be gained otherwise.

•   •   •   •   •

Suppose you're at a cocktail party. You take the risk to approach someone who is standing alone, and you strike up a conversation. You then gather some interesting facets of their story. But will you go a step further and ask a couple of deeper questions about their journey, or will you let things stay superficial and then make a joke to ease the discomfort of your exit as you walk away?

Or perhaps you're returning from a business trip, and halfway into the flight the man seated next to you feels comfortable enough in your conversation to mention he's still reeling from the death of his dad earlier in the year. You remember a book you once read that solidified your own faith after you had walked through a significant season of grief. Will you take the risk to reveal your belief in God and recommend the book, or will you give him a sympathetic nod and then migrate to a different subject?

Standing in your child's classroom at the school holiday party, you overhear the teacher telling another parent that this month will be a little tough since she won't be able to make the trip back east to spend Christmas with her family. Alone for the holidays ... not good. Will you risk inviting her to Christmas Eve services with your family or to your home for a leftovers party after Christmas, or will you act as though you never heard about her situation?

In your day-to-day life, there are countless opportunities where forks in the road like these show up. Situations where you have to declare to yourself and to God whether or not you will take the next step to have impact in people's lives. Here's the bottom line: choosing wisely in these fork-in-the-road moments is what living in 3D is all about.

You don't have to be any more talented, any richer, any slimmer, any smarter, any more or less of *anything* to partner with God. All you have to be is willing to be used by him in everyday ways. If that's true of you, then let's get all over this assignment of learning to discern appropriate next steps in pointing people toward him!

INITIAL INTERACTIONS

I have a friend whose family recently relocated to a new city. A few days after moving in, she met her next-door neighbor. During their brief exchange, the neighbor volunteered a few details about her life: she had four kids and a husband, worked at a large corporation, and struggled to get the work-and-home balance right. Her oldest son—a strong-willed eighteen-year-old, according to her—had graduated from high school but was waffling about whether or not to go to college. He worked as a sacker at the nearby grocery store.

Her family constantly juggled dozens of overlapping activities like baseball games and her husband's business trips, causing their two Labrador retrievers to hang out in the backyard for days on end without attention. After a few minutes of chatter, the two women turned to head toward their respective homes. The dogs ran toward them from the deck, both with tennis balls in their jowls and pleading eyes. "See, this is what I mean," the neighbor said. "They have *way* more energy than our family has time to exhaust. We feel so guilty!" As she walked away, she let out a frustrated laugh that acknowledged the maddening busyness of life.

Now maybe after an encounter like that, you'd politely nod and smile and excuse yourself with, "Well, it was nice to meet you." But what I want you to see is that any typical ten-minute exchange can unearth *dozens* of ways for you to help source the needs of people in your sphere of influence.

Try to catch the crystal-clear signals people send —often unintentionally—that inform you about their needs and that can guide you toward the right

resources to suggest. It doesn't take a genius to discern appropriate next steps in relationships. All it
takes is radar that's simultaneously tracking the Holy
Spirit's promptings as well as the needs of the person
you are talking to.

Maybe it's a timely word or a well-intentioned
question. A thoughtfully chosen book or message or
a fitting seminar or event. A willing spirit, a heartfelt
laugh, a safe ear, or—as my work-from-home friend
discovered—a commitment to taking a couple of
dogs on a run a few afternoons a week while the
family tends to their to-dos. Who knows where that
small, caring act might lead!

It really is true—everyday, seemingly insignifi-
cant things can become divine, life-altering tools in
the hands of compassionate Christ-followers. But
you'll never know their impact until you offer them
up as resources to meet the needs around you.

* * * * ●

I had been on the road for a series of speaking
engagements one winter when I decided to head out
alone to eat breakfast and to spend a few minutes
being still before God. It was blustery and cold that
morning, but I remember feeling warmed by God's
presence while I whispered a prayer as I crossed the
street to enter the café. *Just for today, God, I will do
whatever you ask me to do. Just for today.* I didn't want
to overpromise and underdeliver, so I took the safe

route. Figured I would keep the bar low. "One day. Whatever you ask, God." That was the deal.

A hot meal, several cups of coffee, and forty-five minutes later, I was walking back toward my car, bracing against the blowing snow that was pounding my face. Almost audibly, I received a prompting from God. These don't necessarily flow into my life in a steady stream, but on that particular day, it happened. "Turn around," he prompted.

So, as you might expect, I kept right on walking.

To my dismay, his voice wasn't subdued by my obstinacy. "Turn around," he prompted again. My short-term memory indicted me as I remembered that less than one hour prior, I had promised God that I would be available to him for that entire day. How could I refuse his leading so soon after I'd made such a clear commitment?

I turned to look behind me and saw absolutely nothing there. "See, God?" I sort of sneered. But as I wheeled back around, I saw an elderly woman—probably at least eighty-five—who had been dropped off by a city bus on the corner a few feet in front of me. She was obviously out to take care of some shopping but was stymied by a tall snowbank blockading the entrance to the first store on her list of stops.

"How are you going to get over that snowbank?" My tone told her that I expected to help out.

"It's gonna be tough unless you help me, sonny," she said without missing a beat. Looking down the

street a little, I noticed that the snowy obstacle out-
lined the sidewalk for blocks. I kicked the snow bank
down some and found inches-thick ice underneath.
Even clutching my arm, there was no way she could
step across the bank without slipping.

"Ma'am, I'm not sure how to tell you this, but
the only way I can help you is to lift you over this
thing."

She paused for a moment. "Well I can't stay *here*
all day! Lift away, but you'd better be careful with
me." She loosened her posture as an early sign that
she was ready to trust a complete stranger.

As gently as I could, I lifted her over the snowbank, set her down just outside the store entrance,
and then asked about her transportation once she
had finished her errands. "I'll be just fine, sonny,"
she said with a frail hand on my shoulder. "Thank
you for helping me. You're a nice young man."

I watched her enter the store and continued head-
ing toward my car, still shivering from the wind. It
occurred to me as I drove toward the location of
my first speaking engagement that the simple act
of meeting someone's immediate need that morning would likely trump the more public and intel-
lectually stimulating events of my day. During a few
moments at a stoplight, now in the heated comfort of
my car, I speculated about how it all unfolded.

Here was God sitting up there observing one of
his fragile and aging daughters who needed help on

a frigid winter morning. He knew of this semipli-able, strapping (if I do say so myself) young son who was in the same vicinity. And so he sent a message through the Spirit to alert the son to the need. Sure, it got goofed up and ignored along the way, but finally it came through loud and clear. "Turn around!" he had urged. And finally I had turned around.

In a nutshell, that was the extent of what hap-pened that day. God chose to use me to meet a practi-cal need. And despite its evident simplicity, it served to reaffirm my daily goal as a follower of Christ — to be acutely aware of God's activity in this world and to be willing for him to use me in accomplishing some part of it, be it large or small.

Obviously, I have no idea if that minuscule act of kindness played any role whatsoever in that woman eventually coming to faith in God. Maybe she was already a Christ-follower; I don't know. But the key is to have a willing spirit, an open heart, and a mind-set that says, "If there is absolutely *any* resource I can pro-vide that will ease your burden, untangle your confu-sion, or solidify your trust in the God who built you and loves you, then I hope you'll let me provide it."

THE GOAL OF THE WALK-ACROSS-THE-ROOM PERSON

I have seen firsthand what happens to human lives when Christ takes his rightful place in the heart of an individual. In the home of a family. In the heart of a church. In the seat of a community. The ripple effect of faith is astounding! And do you know where your ripple effect begins? With you walking across a room, listening carefully, and taking next steps to help point people toward God. Meeting a practical need, recommending a good book, praying a prayer —this is where it all begins. And you can do this! You can be the spiritual adrenaline injection for your sphere of influence.

In preparation for our annual elders' retreat one summer, one of our elders secretly went around asking people whose personal lives had been touched by the other elders to write a note of thanks to them, which she then framed and presented as gifts to each one of us. To this day I have no idea how she pulled it off, but somehow she tracked down an old sailing crew buddy of mine named Dave Wright.

Dave's journey to faith was anything but a straight line, but the day finally arrived when he made a powerful decision to begin following Christ—a decision that transformed every nook and cranny of his heart, soul, and life. Talk about a spiritual adrenaline injection for all of us who call ourselves his friends! To this day, he is known by most as "Super Dave," a well-suited moniker for a man with the most expansive heart you'll find. These days, his life influences hundreds of thousands of people as he faithfully serves the Willow Creek Association.

The words he penned in response to the elder's request for the note will stick with me until my dying day. You can read it for yourself—here's the letter that is now framed in my office area.

7/18/99

Bill:

I am a Christian! I owe this to you and God. I am so thankful that you listened when he prompted you to start a sailing team of non-Christians. I sincerely and deeply appreciate your never-ending patience and guidance over the past eight years. Our friendship is priceless to me, and I love you.

For eternity,
Super

Those of you who have known someone on both sides of their faith commitment understand that no trophy, no promotion, no pleasure, no possession will ever hold a candle to the thrill we feel when God uses us to touch another human life for eternity.

* * * * •

At some point, if you are a follower of Christ's, you're going to say your final farewell to this planet and head to heaven for all eternity. When you get there, you'll meet my sailing buddy Dave. You'll also meet a first-century woman who stood thirsty beside a well one afternoon but who had her eternal thirst quenched by the Living Water himself.

You'll meet a former tax collector named Matthew who experienced mind-boggling, in-person adventures with Jesus Christ—as well as a few former tax-collecting friends who had their worlds rocked when the love of Christ invaded their hearts.

If you're like me, you'll probably walk right up to Matthew and ask to hear his radical before-and-after story firsthand. And I just bet that as you approach him, slowing a little because you notice that he's in the middle of a conversation, you'll be overjoyed to discover that the person he's talking to is your friend, your father, your neighbor, your boss, your teacher, your hairstylist, or the owner of your dry-cleaning service.

This is unbelievable! you'll think as you take in the person standing in front of you. You can think of nothing else to ask but the one question that would be on anyone's mind when they find a career sinner on the right side of the pearly gates: "How'd you get here?!"

"You know, I was just a jumble of knots, so twisted up about this whole God-thing," the explanation will begin, "until the day when you walked across that room. *That* day—that was the day things started getting worked out for me."

Experience the Four-Week
Just Walk Across the Room
Church Campaign Today!

Visit *www.justwalkacrosstheroom.com* to access all of the information you need to launch the most life-changing and kingdom-building four-week campaign your church may ever experience.

Resources available to order online:

Curriculum Kit   031027172x
Hardcover   0310266696
Small Group DVD   0310271746
Participant's Guide   0310271762

We want to hear from you. Please send
your comments about this book to us in care of
zreview@zondervan.com. Thank you.